Class

27-2=25 rings